STARTING SQUASH

By Dick Hawkey

© COPYRIGHT 1979 AND PUBLISHED BY
COLES PUBLISHING COMPANY LIMITED
TORONTO — CANADA
PRINTED IN CANADA

Contents

Introduction

More and more people all over the world are arming themselves with a racket and a ball, shutting themselves in a four-walled room and inflicting on themselves the physical demands of an extremely energetic pastime. No other game has ever enjoyed such a vast and continuing expansion, and there is no doubt at all that within a very short time, anyone who does not play Squash will be the exception rather than the rule. This book is aimed at anyone who has never played the game, knows nothing about it, but wants to know what all the fuss is about.

Before we get on to individual requirements, it would be as well to explain why the game has suddenly become so popular. Basically, it has always been popular with those who had an opportunity to play it, but because a court is expensive to build, the number of courts available was pitifully few up to 1960. About that time the game, which was by then over a hundred years old, took on a new lease of life. Many outdoor athletic clubs realized that by building courts and having their premises used in the off-season they could save themselves from going bankrupt, and even make a handsome profit. Once this financial aspect became evident, the commercial operators came along and built centres, which opened the game up to the general public, and provided a generous return on capital. And so, suddenly, Squash was available to people who had never heard of it before.

All this happened at a time when the pressures of modern life demanded a game which would give maximum exercise in the minimum time, at a reasonable cost, at any time of day or night, in any weather and without having

to organize teams. Squash passed all the tests. So much
for the 'weight watchers', but what about the serious
games players, who wanted to play something competitively? Squash passed this test too. Indeed, one of the
problems of the rule makers is to curb those who want
to play too competitively! Certainly nowadays there are
enough leagues, championships, representative matches
and overseas tours for the most ambitious spirit, and there
are ever-increasing rewards for getting to the top.

So far so good, but how difficult is this game to learn
and can anyone play? One of its great attractions is that
virtually anyone who is reasonably fit can go on to a court
and within a very short time become fairly proficient.

Above all, the game is fun at all levels; if it were not,
even with all the assets mentioned above, it would not be
attracting people in such large numbers. So if anyone
reads this who has not yet played, now is the time to
start.

You need a court, a racket, a ball and some guidance on
the rules and how to play. You may already know of a
court or club in your area, in which case go along and say
you are thinking of starting to play, and go and watch a
game on one of the courts. If you have a friend who plays,
get him (or her) to take you along and show you the
ropes. Most clubs have rackets they will lend or rent, to
save you the expense of buying one before you discover
whether or not you like the game, and a ball is not an
expensive item. If you do not know of any courts
nearby, contact the Squash Rackets Association **and**

ask for the address of your nearest club or centre, or contact your local Sports Council for details. The latter will also tell you when the next coaching course starts for beginners, if you do decide to take up the game. The one other thing you must have is a pair of shoes that will not mark the floor of the court. All clubs ban black-soled shoes, so do not antagonize everyone on your first visit by leaving black skid marks all over the place.

The chapters that follow are intended to help you spend your time profitably once you are on the court. Because so many complete newcomers are starting the game, I make no apology for starting at Square Minus One!

I

First time on court – the basic rules – the grip – positioning the feet – elementary practice

Beginners in Squash vary from people who have had previous experience with ball games and have already developed a sense of co-ordination, to those who have never played a ball game in their life. Obviously, a coach would be wasting a great deal of his own and the pupil's time if he began his instruction at the same point. People who are already familiar with games such as Tennis or Hockey do have an advantage during the initial stages of learning Squash, but for the benefit of those who do not have this experience, I shall be starting right from the beginning, as a thorough understanding of the aims and techniques provides the basis for developing the skill of the game.

Let us start with just a very basic look at the rules, so that the beginner has a rough idea about what he is aiming to do. The door into the court is almost always in the back wall, so that the high wall facing us is the front wall. The two side walls are the right-hand and left-hand walls (not forehand and backhand, because this would be confusing for left-handers). At the bottom of the front wall is the 'tin' with its 'board' above it, and around all four walls is a red line, known as the 'out-of-court' line. The game is similar to other racket games, like Lawn

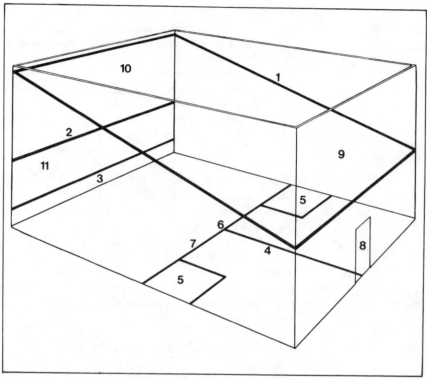

Tennis, Badminton and Table Tennis, in that one player serves, and rallies develop as each player takes alternate shots, until one of them fails to return the ball correctly. This, as in Lawn Tennis, can happen by the ball being hit out of court, by its bouncing twice on the floor before being returned, or by the player hitting the ball into the 'net'. The equivalent of the 'net' in Squash is the tin and the board, and any time the ball touches either of these, the rally is at an end. To be 'out-of-court' at Squash the ball has to hit a wall on or above the out-of-court line, or anything in the roof. The equivalent to a correct Tennis return over the net is striking the ball so that it hits the front wall between the board and the out-of-court line.

The layout of a Squash court.
1 Out-of-court line
2 'Cut' line
3 Tin
4 Half-court line
5 Service box
6 The 'T'
7 'Short' line
8 Door
9 Back wall
10 Front wall
11 Board

Very simply, it is a game in which one player tries to hit the ball against a wall more accurately than his opponent. All the other lines apply only to the service, so we can forget them for the moment, and the side and back walls make no difference to the rally, as the ball can strike them on its way to or from the front wall.

The first essential then is to practise hitting the ball against a wall as often as possible. You will find that there are four different speeds of ball, marked by coloured dots. The slowest is the Yellow, then, going upwards, the White, Red and Blue. 'Professional' players use the Yellow, because their constant hard hitting warms the ball up, and causes it to bounce satisfactorily, but beginners cannot achieve this effect, and should use one of the faster balls, the Red or the Blue.

Now, what about the racket? There is less difference in weight than with Tennis rackets, and there is a large selection of rackets to choose from. It may well be that you just have to use the only racket available, or the one your friend is lending you, but if you do decide to buy one, there are a number of excellent, moderately-priced rackets, which are perfectly satisfactory for your early days in Squash. Later on, if and when you begin serious match play, you can begin thinking about the super rackets. It is more difficult to control shots if your racket is very highly strung, and if one of your early swings causes the frame to break because you have hit the wall hard, it is not such a disaster as if you were picking up the fragments of a racket two or three times as expensive. All you want is a racket that feels comfortable to you. You will find that handles vary in size, and that these are either made of various types of leather or similar materials, or of towelling. The latter is for people who find their hands sweat a lot, and helps them grip the racket better. Others find that it has the reverse effect; it tends to become knotted and hard, and the actual grip varies slightly depending on whether you have a new piece of towelling on it or not. Everyone must decide for himself.

We now come to the question of how to grip the racket. The orthodox grip is achieved by 'shaking hands' with the handle of the racket when it is held towards you as shown in the illustration. Because the racket itself is light, and the ball also light, there are considerable variations in the grip, both in the positioning of the fingers and in the part of the handle actually held. It is up to each individual to decide what suits him or her best, but the vital thing to remember is that in Squash one just does not have time to change one's grip for the backhand, so however the racket is held, it must be convenient and comfortable for both types of swing. Squash is a game where the wrist plays a major part in stroke production, so the grip must allow freedom of movement to the wrist as well as the arm.

Quite frequently, a player who is new to racket games finds it difficult to make contact with the ball. This is perfectly understandable, because the eye and hand are reasonably co-ordinated after a lifetime of touching things,

Two beginners 'shaking hands' with the racket to achieve the correct grip. If this is done at the angle shown, the racket head is automatically 'up', and in the correct position.

but the eye is not yet geared to an extension of the arm. If, therefore, a player does find he has an initial problem, the best way to overcome it is to put the ball on the racket, and hold it out at arm's length. By playing around with it, bouncing it up and down and making sure it does not fall, the eye will get used to seeing ball and racket in contact, and make the adjustments necessary to hit the ball in future.

A beginner getting his eye accustomed to the racket and ball being in contact by balancing the ball on the racket, prior to bouncing it up and down.

We now are on court with a racket and ball for the first time. The people new to racket games have got used to bouncing the ball on the racket and everyone is ready to start Squash. As I said earlier, it is a game in which the player who hits the ball more accurately against the wall will win, so we must begin practising hitting the ball against the wall. At this stage, I do not think it matters how this is done. Throughout coaching it is essential to build on confidence and what the player can do competently.

If, at this stage, a coach were to insist on all the details of correct foot positioning, perfect, full racket swinging, and transferring the weight of the body forwards during the shot, all he would achieve is a feeling of despair in the pupil, who would have so much on his mind that he certainly would not hit the ball. Far better to let the player hit the ball up and down to himself a number of times, and then gradually correct the faults one by one, so that he only has a single point at a time to worry about as he continues to hit the ball.

First of all then, go up as close as you like to the front wall, and see how often you can keep a little rally going by yourself, either volleying the ball gently against the wall, or allowing it to bounce once on the floor. When you can maintain a rally of fifteen shots, move back several feet from your original position, and continue your practice until you can keep fifteen shots going from there.

Up to now we have not worried about the positioning of the feet, but it is now time to think about this. There are a

The first knock-up. The beginner on the left is still concentrating on keeping the ball going, whereas the one on the right has progressed as far as getting his feet in the correct position.

In illustration A the feet are placed facing the front wall. As the racket is swinging across the line of the ball (indicated by the arrows), it has a limited time in which contact is made and is almost certain to hit the ball across court. In illustrations B and C the feet are placed so that the body is facing the side wall, giving a much longer period in which the racket is travelling along the path of the approaching ball and thereby increasing the chances of returning the ball parallel to the side walls. In the illustrations the player is assumed to be right-handed.

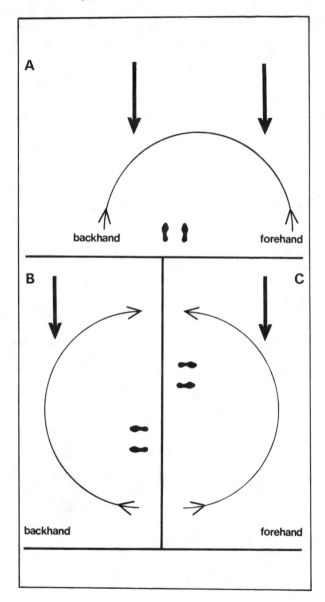

A

backhand   forehand

B   C

backhand   forehand

number of reasons why it is important to get it right. In the first place, the natural swing of the racket arm is from the far flung position, level with the shoulder, round in an arc to a position across the chest. The illustrations show that a racket held in an arm moving through this arc would be most likely to strike a ball moving parallel with the chest. It follows then that as most shots in Squash will be played as they return down the court from the front wall, the body must be so placed that the chest is parallel to the ball's line of flight, so that the racket may have the maximum chance of making contact. To do this, the feet must be placed so that they are pointing towards the side wall, enabling the stroke to be played naturally and without contortion, and of course this is true for both forehand and backhand shots.

The second reason for correct foot positioning is that it is important in Squash to base one's game on strokes parallel with the side walls, and preferably strokes which send the ball into the back corners of the court. The reason is that a player may often mishit a ball if he is forced to play it close to a wall, and may be unable to retrieve it at all if he has to try and dig it out of a back corner, impeded by the closeness of the back wall as well as the side wall. It also means that he has to move a long way, if he is continually made to play shots from the extremities of the court, and this will in time tire him out. It can be seen from the diagrams that the only places where a player who is facing the front wall can hit the ball back parallel to the side walls are at the extreme beginnings of his forehand or backhand swings. In this case there would certainly not be enough momentum for the ball to be hit hard enough to carry to the rear of the court. If hit anywhere else in the swing, the ball must be struck across court.

The third reason is that Squash offers a very much wider range of shots than any of the other racket games in which there are no walls. Instead of merely hitting the ball down a narrow avenue more or less straight ahead, as in Lawn Tennis, one can make a good return by hitting it in any

The intention (*left*) was to play a backhand down the wall. What actually happened (*right*)—the opponent was given an easy shot in the centre of the court.

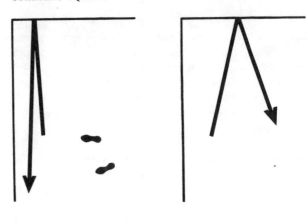

The reasons for this are shown under A, B and C:
A Ball struck in front of the leading foot
B Wrist giving wrong angle to racket
C Feet wrong

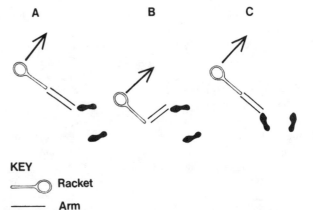

KEY

⊸◯ **Racket**

═══ **Arm**

direction, and by deliberate and accurate use of the side walls, one can deceive and wrong-foot one's opponent. Such strokes are known as 'angles', and are an important part of the game. It would be well nigh impossible to hit the ball into the nearer side wall with one's feet facing the front wall.

These points may be obvious, but it is as well for the beginner to observe them in the initial stages as they play an important part in developing the skills of the game.

On this, and the following
pages, are illustrated the
three reasons why a
backhand shot, intended
to go down the wall,
may go across court.
Here, the ball has been
struck well in front of the
right foot.

A little further on I will be amending the foot positions
shown in the diagrams to the final best position from which
all the normal strokes can be produced most easily, but
the aim at present is to encourage players to take up the
sideways-on position when practising the basic shots of the
game.

You will now be able to keep rallies going, and able to
play both forehand and backhand rallies from the correct
foot position. If you are on your own, set yourself targets

Although the ball has been struck opposite the leading foot, the wrist has advanced the head of the racket, so that the ball is flicked over to the forehand side.

of a certain number of shots up and down the court returning between your own body and the side wall, remembering to give more time to the side you find more difficult; this will probably be the backhand, but not necessarily so. In Squash, it is vital never to run round a backhand; not only does one usually not have time to do so, but if one does, it opens up the whole of the forehand side of the court for the opponent to play a winner. You

Here, the feet are facing the front wall and it would be virtually impossible to hit the ball parallel with the wall.

must, therefore, eliminate any backhand weaknesses very early on. There is no reason why it should not be every bit as strong as the forehand; it is in fact a more natural stroke, as one is 'unwinding' the body rather than 'closing' it, with the forehand bringing the arm across the chest. In fact, among top-ranking players, those whose backhands are more powerful and more accurate than their forehands are as numerous as those whose forehand is the stronger side.

As your solitary practice continues, it is a good idea to station yourself in the centre of the court, hitting alternate forehands and backhands. This is still an accuracy practice, but it involves moving the feet each time. Aim to hit the ball, quite gently at first, so that it returns a comfortable distance away on the other side of your body, and only speed up as you begin to do this successfully.

If you are lucky enough to have someone to play with, you can practise either the shots up and down the side wall, or across court. However, now we are talking about two players on court for the first time, we must stress the safety requirements of Squash. People who have come to Squash from sports where their opponents are safely positioned some distance away the other side of a net, do not always realize that now there is a wall where the net usually is. It is only too easy for the beginner, in his eagerness to reach a shot, to inadvertently hit his opponent rather than the ball. It is absolutely essential that this point is realized right from the start; never play a shot if there is the slightest risk of hitting the other player with your racket. Far better to refrain from playing a stroke, unless you are quite sure that your opponent is safely out of your reach. It is also desirable to avoid hitting an opponent with the ball; the rules cover these situations, and also allow a referee to give the appropriate decision when a player refrains from playing a ball for fear of hitting the other player. So do not run risks; very serious injuries can result from thoughtlessness or dangerous use of the racket.

Quite apart from the undesirability of being known as a menace on the court, a big racket swing is actually detrimental to one's efficiency as a Squash player. I have said before how fast the game is, and one simply does not have enough time to take a full-arm backswing, or recover from a long follow-through. It is a light racket and a light ball, and all the power one needs can be obtained from the wrist, so cut down on any scythe-like swing you may find yourself developing; accuracy and speed of shot count for far more in Squash, and you find yourself with more willing partners than the person who handles his racket like a quarterstaff.

The two basic practices for you and your partner, before we go on to the various strokes, are as follows. To practise the shots up and down the side wall, take up position around the centre of one of the rear quarters of the court, and aim to hit the ball up on to the front wall so that it returns into the same area. As you finish your stroke, back away towards the centre of the court, allowing your partner a clear view of the approaching ball and an un-impeded shot at it, and then move in behind him again for your turn, once he has played. It is always a good idea to make practices competitive, as it prevents them from becoming boring, and is good preparation for the highly competitive games and matches to come. At this stage points should be lost by the player who causes the rally to break down, either by failing to return the ball correctly, or by hitting it in such a way that his partner had no chance of returning it. Remember that the practice is equally valuable on both sides of the court, and the time available should be sensibly divided between forehand and backhand.

The other useful practice at this stage is for the players to stand just behind the 'short' line, which is the line parallel with the front wall, dividing the court into a front and rear half. One stands in the centre of the forehand side of the court, and the other similarly on the backhand. They must then hit the ball so that the partner can take it on the correct side, forehand from the forehand side and backhand from the backhand. Again, the rally is lost by the person causing the rally to come to an end. Remember to divide the available time equally, so that each player gets his fair share on each side of the court.

When these two practices can be carried out successfully, we are ready to move on to the various strokes used in Squash and basic 'tactics'.

2

Footwork and racket swing – the basic strokes – the drive – the lob – the drop shot – the angle – volleying

I want to start this chapter by going on with the idea of correct footwork, so that we can proceed to discuss the various shots in Squash. The sideways-on position in Chapter 1 was an 'L' driver's piece of instruction and is good enough for the practices suggested so far, but it is only a halfway house. The optimum position for all the shots, when you have time to get into that position, is even further round than the 'facing-the-side-wall' position. This means that the leading foot (for a right hander's forehand the left foot), should be closer to the side wall than the rear foot, and as the shot is played, the weight is brought forward on to the front foot, and the ball struck more or less opposite that foot. I say 'more or less' because a player may hit the ball early (before it reaches a position level with the foot) or late, in order to alter the direction in which the ball is struck.

The advantages of this position are that the racket has now gained its full momentum in the swing, the wrist has full freedom and, with the weight being transferred forward, maximum power and control over the ball can be exercised.

So much for the footwork; we must now improve the racket swing. So far we have used a full wide Tennis-like

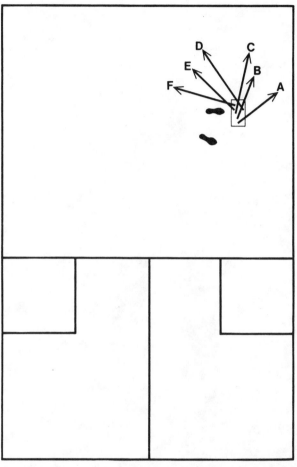

For a right-handed player the following shots are possible from this position:

A Forehand angle shot
B Forehand drop shot
C Lob or drive into back forehand corner
D Cross-court lob (drive played a little wider)
E Cross-court drop shot
F Reverse angle shot, returning to front forehand corner

All are played from the area shown as a rectangle opposite the front foot. The various angles can be achieved either by use of the wrist, or by taking the ball early (in front of the foot) or late (after it has passed it).

swing, but in Squash this does not work because there is not time to take the racket back that far. Also, the ball may do something rapid and surprising, which would elude a player whose racket was just starting on its wide arc. Furthermore, the referee and one's opponent will object sooner or later on safety grounds. The correct approach position is with the racket held well up, the racket head high and the wrist 'cocked', ready to whip the racket head at the ball. By

Here, and overleaf, are illustrated the backswing, stroke and follow-through for the correct backhand shot. Note eyes on the ball as it approaches, is struck and departs.

correct use of the wrist, a long and violent arm action is not necessary. Throughout the shot, the racket head should be above the wrist; the lower the ball, the lower the player should bend to make this possible. It is not good Squash to drop the racket head and play with the racket trailing. The follow-through should again be short, in the interests of

The ball is struck level with the front foot, and the weight is transferred to the front foot as the shot is played.

safety as well as economy of movement, and any impetus that has to be taken up after a powerful shot should be directed upwards at the end of the swing, not round past the front shoulder, where the opponent may be.

The skill, therefore, that every player needs to acquire as early as he can, is to gauge the approach of the ball from an

The backswing and
follow-through are kept
close to the body and are
no danger to an opponent.

opponent's stroke, and work out where it will be possible
for him to meet the ball, so that he is in this correct position
and able to unleash his full range of strokes at it. This intro-
duces another factor, which is the ability to judge the flight
of a Squash ball. In the other games a ball is flying more or
less directly towards you, and you have only to judge its
speed of approach. Unless you get an unlucky bounce, it
will not deviate. A Squash ball, on the other hand, is very
likely to be rebounding off one or two walls on its way,

and one frequently sees beginners running into a ball which has been hit into a side wall, and which, if they stood still, would arrive at a very convenient place to be struck. As a result, they have no room to play a shot, and are either hit by the ball, or hit themselves with the racket. Equally, one often sees a player waiting for the ball to rebound from a side wall, only to misjudge it completely, and find that it has remained much closer to the wall than he expected. Consequently, the ball does not come within his range at all. Obviously players must learn how to judge the behaviour of the ball when it strikes the side or back wall, in order to assess where best to play it. Only experience will give them this knowledge and enable them to move instinctively to the right place. Good players do this automatically, and the skill is taken for granted, but it is not an art that comes readily to all beginners.

It is important, therefore, to follow the two very basic practices of the last chapter, where the ball was being hit straight up and down the court, or directly across to a partner, in neither case using any wall other than the front, with a practice in which the ball is hit deliberately against a side wall either on its way to or from the front wall. A player on his own can stand near the centre of the court, and hit the ball towards the front corner of the court, so that it returns via the front and side walls. He will notice that when he mishits it on to the side wall first, the ball will then go further across court than the one hitting the front wall first, which will come further down the court. Experiments in this will build experience.

There are two tips that may be worth remembering: the first is that the ball should leave a wall at the corresponding angle to its approach, providing the wall surface is true and dry; and secondly, that if a ball hits the wall before bouncing on the floor, it will come away from that wall far further than if it bounces first and then hits the wall. If, therefore, you can judge which it will do first, bounce on the floor or hit a wall, you can learn to judge whether to move in to the ball, or stand back and wait for it to come to you. This fact also affects the way one plays the various strokes; if the aim is to draw the opponent into a corner of the court, or close to a side wall, then the ball must be made to bounce before hitting a wall. It also makes life more difficult for an opponent, especially in the case of a hard-hit shot, when things are happening quickly, if the ball is struck towards the crack where the wall and floor join, known as the 'nick'. If the ball lands right in the nick, it is liable to roll straight along the floor and be impossible to retrieve, but even if the ball is somewhere near the nick, it gives very little time for the opponent to guess what it will do. This is perhaps a rather advanced piece of instruction for the complete beginner, but it follows directly from the discussion on side wall shots, and will save explanations later on, when we are discussing how and why to play certain shots.

As we said earlier, there is a much wider range of strokes in Squash than in most other similar games. Basically there are four, not counting the service, which is a little different. These four are the drive, the lob, the drop and the angle. As these can be played on the forehand or backhand, this makes eight, and as they can be hit to either side of the court, the total is sixteen. However, only eight are possible on each occasion, and then only when the ball is clear of the walls. This is because the shot must be either a forehand or a backhand; it cannot be both, so the sixteen are immediately halved. The nearness of a wall or walls can obviously inhibit certain shots, because the racket is not able to have a free swing.

Let us explain first of all what the various shots are before looking at them in detail, and before talking about the advantages in playing each. The drive is a hard-hit shot, normally aimed to pass the opponent, and to land in one of the back corners of the court. The lob is a shot hit high and over the head of the opponent, with the same aim as the drive, namely to embarrass the opponent in the rear of the court. Both these strokes need to be played to what is known in Squash as a 'good length'. This means that they should be hit in such a way that the opponent is in two minds whether to take the ball before it reaches the back wall, or to allow it to hit the back wall, and hope it will rebound far enough to be retrieved. It means that the ball will be bouncing for the second time close to the back wall, whether this is before or after striking the wall. Obviously it cannot be a 'good length' if the ball hits the back wall direct, because, as we already learned when discussing the behaviour of a ball striking any wall, it will rebound further from that wall if it has not already bounced on the floor, so the second bounce would then be well out in the court again, offering the opponent an easy shot.

The drop shot has the opposite aim from the drive and the lob; it aims to make life difficult for the opponent in the front corner of the court. The various angle shots are shots which hit a side wall on their way to the front wall, and can be used to make a surprise alteration in the direction of the ball which will deceive the opponent, and may well catch him going the wrong way.

A Squash court may appear a very large place at first when you are just learning the game, and some sadistic friend is standing in the middle of the court making you run in all directions to pick up his shots, but as you improve, and begin playing longer rallies against other competent players, the court will seem to have shrunk. It will seem a very difficult task to put the ball anywhere in the court where your opponent cannot get to it. His ability to do so will depend very largely on how easy he finds it to anticipate your strokes. If you have a limited repertoire, it will make his task of anticipation that much easier, but if you have, and use, all eight shots on both forehand and backhand, he may well guess wrong or have to wait until you have played the shot before he can move off towards it. So it is important to have the full range of shots on both sides of the court, and to use them, so that your opponent cannot guess what is coming.

Every time you play a stroke in Squash, whatever type of stroke it is, you should have a definite aim in view. I suppose the aim can be divided into defensive or aggressive, with a lot of 'no-man's-land' in between. If we take the range as being from nought to a hundred, the nought position would be a desperate last-minute lunge at a ball in the forlorn hope of getting it back somehow, and the hundred spot would be occupied by a shot aimed at being an outright winner, such as a drop shot to a front corner with the opponent well out of position in the back of the court. In between are the wide range of shots which can be both aggressive and defensive at the same time. For example, a player forced to retrieve a good drop shot in the front of the court may well decide that his best method of defence is to lob, but if he has time to play the shot well, it might easily turn the tables completely and prove a very good attacking stroke by landing in the opposite rear corner of the court. Similarly, a player may have a good attacking position in the front of the court, and may wish to play an aggressive shot. However, he does not know where his opponent is, and the score at that moment is such that he cannot afford to take any risks, so he wisely decides to blend attack with caution, and plays a shot which is completely safe and which will push the opponent into the back corners. It is unlikely to be a winner but it will keep the rally going and retain the initiative. Frequently, too, the tactical situation will affect the choice of shot. A very fit player may well not want to run the risk of hitting a ball down, even when in the perfect position to play a likely winner, and may opt for a good length shot to keep the rally going and tire his opponent; this could be termed aggression by defence. The point I am hoping to make is the importance of being able to play all the shots so that one can deceive one's opponent, attack or defend as necessary, play the ball to any part of the court and always have a shot for any situation.

Let us now return to the basic position we were discussing earlier, and starting from that, discuss how to produce the various shots. First of all, the drive. Let us assume we are approaching the ball with the racket held high, getting into the position that will enable the ball to be hit as it comes level with the front foot. As the front foot lands, the weight is transferred on to it, and the arm and wrist bring the racket head through, and contact is made opposite that foot. The usual aim is to hit the ball hard down the court as near as possible and parallel to the nearest side wall. The object is to achieve a good length, and it will depend on the speed of the ball and the temperature of the court where

Here, and overleaf, are illustrated a variety of possible shots in the front forehand corner. This photograph shows the basic position, from which the opponent has no possible way of anticipating what is coming.

Sig. 3

the ball should strike the front wall. The faster the ball and the hotter the court, the lower the ball can be hit, and still reach the back of the court on its second bounce. Indeed, if in these circumstances the ball is hit upwards on to the front wall, it will rebound too far from the back wall to be effective. However, in cold conditions, when the ball is

Here, the wrist has been opened to produce an angle shot.

much 'deader', the ball needs to be hit upwards on to the
front wall for there to be any hope that it will carry to the
back. The point about hitting the ball parallel to the side
wall, is that you double your chances of setting the opponent a problem. Even if the ball is not hit to a good length,
it will not be easy for him to play anything very aggressive

This picture shows the
follow-through after
a lob.

if he is forced to play the ball within a few inches of the side wall, and sooner or later, if you continue to play this shot, one will cling to the side wall and be difficult to return at all. Of course, if you can keep the ball close to the wall and to a good length as well, you are really putting pressure on him.

If the drive is hit across court, it should only be because you have a particular reason for doing so. When we get on to the subject of tactics and movement around the court, I will explain that it is important to move to the centre of the court between shots, so we can assume that the opponent is standing in the centre of the court. Therefore, if the cross-court drive is only slightly mishit, it will offer him a chance to play the ball into an open part of the court for a winner. This should always be borne in mind when hitting the ball hard; if you mishit it, or the opponent anticipates correctly, the ball is on his racket too quickly for you to have recovered your position. It is often a fault that beginners, and even quite experienced players, make when they are trying to speed the game up; they hit too hard and sacrifice accuracy. As a result, they are only speeding themselves up, and not their opponent. However, provided that is all remembered, the cross-court drive, aimed to hit the opposite wall in the service box area, can be a useful shot, and a useful variety to the regular stream of drives down the wall.

The drives can be played from any part of the court, provided you are not close to a wall; obviously, it is not good sense to aim to hit the ball hard, if there is a risk of hitting the wall with the racket. It is most usefully played from the centre or rear of the court, when the aim is to keep the rally going safely by playing a shot which will ensure that the opponent has no chance of attempting a winner. It can be played from the front of the court, but very often there is something more ambitious and aggressive that one can attempt from there, and always the risk of being caught out of position if the opponent gets to the drive and hits it past you, before you can move.

The next shot, the lob, has the same basic aim as the

drive, but is played very differently. The aim is embarrassment in the rear corners, and the method is by hitting the
ball upwards, so that it will fall as near vertically as possible
in the back of the court. The more steeply it can be made
to drop, and the less 'way' it has on it, the less it will rebound from the back wall; it has, therefore, a much better
chance than a drive of being a 'good length' shot. It is
easiest to play a lob accurately from the front of the court,
but it can be played from anywhere. It can form part of a
deliberate plan to slow the game down, or provide a sudden
change of pace or be used as a tactic against an opponent
who has revealed a weakness in his overhead shots. To hit
the ball up in the air, it is necessary to get the racket under
the ball and play it upwards on to the front wall, so that it
continues to rise and pass high over the centre of the court
and out of the reach of the opponent's racket. The lob is
most effective played across court, unlike the drive, so this
point about being over the opponent's reach is an important one. The reason for playing it across court is that it
should then hit the side wall just below the out-of-court
line, well back in the court, and then bounce on the floor
before striking the back wall. The impact against the side
wall, floor or back wall, will further reduce the speed of a
fairly slow-moving ball, and it is likely that it will not
emerge far enough from that wall for the opponent to get
it back. If the lob is played down the wall, the ball only
glances along the side wall, is barely slowed up by it, so
hits the back wall more directly, and will therefore rebound
further. The vital factor which determines whether you
can play lobs successfully or not is the height of the court
roof. New courts are normally built nowadays with
18 feet 6 inches or 19 feet clearance below all lights, beams
and other impediments. There are, however, a number of
courts where this amount of roof space has not been provided, either to save money, or because of some building
restriction imposed on the courts by the fact that they have
been built in the basement or centre of some vast hotel or
office block. There are also old courts with an interesting

variety of beams, rafters and swinging lanterns which may
be essential to hold the court together and illuminate it, but
are death to the lob. So before you start lobbing, do have a
look at the roof, and in particular the part about one third
of the way back from the front wall, where most lobs are
reaching their highest point. Make sure you have room for
the shot.

The actual playing of the shot depends again on the basic
position, but in order to get the required elevation, the
ball should be hit well in front of the leading foot, in order
to get under the ball, and hit it on the upward part of the
swing. It is usual to want to hit a low ball, such as an opponent's drop shot, as a lob, and the knees and body must bend
in order to enable the racket to get under the ball without
dropping the racket into a vertical position. It is not a hard-
hit shot, but an 'up-and-under'; if played too hard, it will
hit the back wall without bouncing, and present the
opponent with an easy return.

The lob has two bonuses; one is that, because it is not a
hard-hit shot, the opponent cannot be sure until the last
minute that you are not going to play a drop shot (and
so has to be close enough to the front corner in case you do).
This makes the surprise lob into the back corner even more
awkward for him as he has a long way to travel, and cannot
cut the ball off. Secondly, it forces an opponent to look up
and sight the ball against a background of the roof and the
lights. Rather like the question of the height of the roof,
modern courts tend to be well designed and have clear,
well-lit ceiling backgrounds, but some courts have a background like the catacombs or a modern art masterpiece and
timing a small black object against it is far from easy. So the
lob is used to get you out of trouble in the front of the
court, and give you time to recover, but it can also be a
very effective method of attacking, and is a shot well worth
perfecting.

Next, the drop shot. This, more than the others we have
discussed so far, is almost always an attacking stroke. It is
used to play a winner in the front of the court, and should

normally be played from a position in front of the 'short' line, when the opponent is behind you. In this way, the opponent is forced to move round you to try and get to the ball before it bounces twice. In his eagerness to do so, he may commit himself too early, and begin to move up on your right or left. Provided you are in the correct position, it is then possible to change the direction of your shot, if necessary, by playing the ball to the other side of the court, either by playing a cross-court drop or an angle, or even switching to a lob or drive. Once again, we see the advantages of the correct basic position and the need to have a range of strokes. However, this possible need to change the shot at the last minute emphasises the importance of playing the shot in the orthodox way. The drop needs to be accurate, or it can become a loser and not a winner, either because it goes into the tin, or sets up a very easy shot for the opponent. Do not play speculative drops, the percentages are against you. Wait until you are on balance and in position, and can play the shot properly, and be as sure as you can that your opponent is so placed that he is going to find it difficult to get to. Obviously the front of the court is the most dangerous place to give anyone a free hit, because there is so much less time to anticipate what they are going to do, and such a wide range of winners is open to them. A poor drop shot is the best way of setting your opponent up for a winner, and a poor drop shot played when the opponent is not out of position is the Squash equivalent of suicide! It is a shot that requires steadiness of hand and nerve, and a lot of practice.

The mechanics of a drop shot are much like the drive, except that the ball is guided towards the front wall, and not hit. It is still a full stroke, and not a push or jab at the ball, and has the normal back-swing and follow-through. However, the wrist is not 'whipping' the ball, as in the drive, and it is played with a more deliberate and less rapid arm action. You should be moving forward to play the ball because it will be in your interest to hit it as early as possible. This is partly because the closer to the front wall

you hit it, the easier it is to hit it accurately since the ball
has less far to travel, and partly because it will shorten the
time your opponent has to get to it. Thus there is no problem about getting into the correct position, with the weight
moving forward. Ideally, the ball is easiest to play when it
is at the top of its bounce, or just after it, but circumstances
may require you to adapt this. Keep the racket head up,
bend if necessary to achieve this, and guide the ball towards
the front wall. The aim is to hit the front wall just above
the board, so that it will rebound towards the side-wall
'nick'. Remember, it is preferable to hit the floor before the
side wall, if you do not manage the nick. The most likely
winner, unless you can hear in advance that your opponent
is coming up quickly in the right direction, is when the
drop is played to the nearer front corner. Not only has the
ball a shorter distance to travel, but the racket is not having
to hit across the line of the ball, and both these factors tend
to make it easier to play the 'straight' drop more accurately.
One very important point to remember is that you should
move away quickly after playing the shot, in order to give
your opponent a chance to see and get to the ball, and play
whatever shot he wishes to. This is particularly true with
a drop shot, because the very nature of the stroke means
that the player and the ball are all fairly close in the re-
stricted space of a front corner, and the first movement
must be away towards the middle of the court, before moving back to the centre position.

The other shot to be discussed is the angle, so called because the ball approaches the front wall at an angle, having
been struck against a side wall on the way. Let us discuss
the three categories into which this type of stroke falls. The
name 'angle', as well as being the family name for any shot
striking a side wall first, is also specifically used to describe
an attacking shot, normally played in the front of the court
against the side wall nearer to the player. A 'reverse angle'
is an attacking shot, also usually played well up the court,
in which the ball is pulled across court to strike the side
wall further from the striker. An angle used defensively to

retrieve a ball in the back corners of the court is known as a 'boast', because the ball is either too far past the player, or too close in to the back corner, for him to be able to get it back by any shot direct to the front wall. It must therefore be 'boosted' or 'boasted' on to a side wall for it to carry to the front.

Let us examine these shots. Played aggressively, the angle and reverse angle are effective when produced as surprise

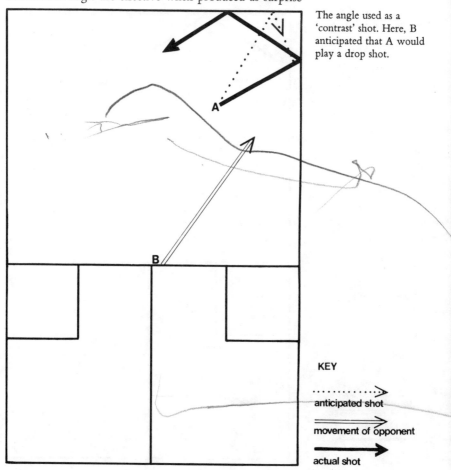

The angle used as a 'contrast' shot. Here, B anticipated that A would play a drop shot.

KEY

⋯⋯⋯⋯⋯▷
anticipated shot

⇒
movement of opponent

➤
actual shot

STARTING SQUASH

alternatives to an expected stroke. For example, if a player has been driving the ball to a good length down his forehand wall from a position in the front forehand corner of the court, the opponent may have begun to assume that this is going to be his normal stroke from such a situation, and to move accordingly towards the back forehand corner. At that moment, the player suddenly produces an angle shot hit hard into the forehand side wall and rebound-

Here, B anticipated that A would play a drive to a length.

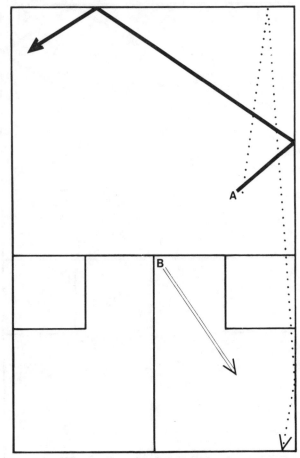

KEY

· · · · · · · · · · · · · · >
anticipated shot

movement of opponent

actual shot

ing towards the front wall and the front backhand corner, and completely catches the opponent. Similarly, a player who has been hitting backhand drives across court, may well find a reverse angle to be a winner. As his opponent is moving to the back forehand corner for yet another cross-court drive, the player pulls the ball even further over, so that it hits the forehand side wall first and rebounds towards the front backhand corner, the one diametrically

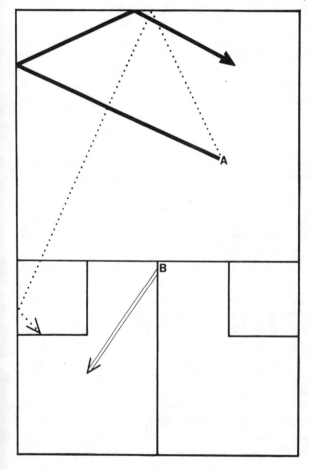

A plays a reverse angle; the anticipated shot was a cross-court drive.

opposite to the one the opponent was anticipating. How are these shots played? Obviously, because they are attempts at surprise winners, the opponent must not be given any advance notice that they are coming, so it is vital that the approach to the ball and the basic position are just the same as for all the other shots. The variety can be introduced either by use of the wrist or by hitting the ball in front of or behind the leading foot, or by a combination of both. It is easy to see how this works; if the ball is hit level with the front foot and the wrist is straight, the ball will be hit parallel with the side wall. If the wrist is bent backwards at that moment, the racket will lag behind the arm and the ball will be hit at the side wall, and similarly if the wrist is advanced, the racket will be ahead of the arm, and the ball will go across court. The same effect is obtained by actually striking the ball in front of or behind the foot with a straight wrist. However, an extreme change of direction, such as a reverse angle near the front wall, when the ball has to be hit almost directly across the court, can only be achieved by use of the wrist and taking the ball well forward of the foot.

For defensive play, the boast has to be used when the ball cannot be hit straight to the front wall. It may be because the ball has been hit past you, in such a way that it will not rebound from the rear wall and has to be hit before it gets there. The only possibility is to hit the ball up on to the side wall and hope it will carry to the front of the court. Once again the ball has to be played on the same principle as the other angles, by using the wrist and a striking position ahead of the front foot. The only thing that is not the same now, is that the feet are placed differently relative to the front wall. How far round you need to face will depend on exactly how far behind you the ball has gone. Initially, I suggest you practise with your feet placed so that they, and you, are facing the back wall in a position near one of the service boxes. You would then be in the correct position to play a drive straight at that side wall. The problem is to get the ball to the front wall, so you have to change your drive by hitting the ball well in front of the foot, and advancing the wrist, just as for the reverse angle. As the side wall will take a lot of the speed from the shot, you need to hit the ball upwards against it, so that it will carry further. A quite gentle upward flick will be more likely to get there than a flat hard drive which will have no chance.

Once the ball can be returned from this position, let us prepare for worse situations, and move the leading foot

Here, and overleaf, are illustrated the correct position for boasting the ball out of the back backhand corner; the feet are facing the opposite corner, so that the front foot can be moved towards the centre of the court should the ball rebound further than anticipated from the side wall. This picture shows the backswing, with the racket held well up and eyes on the ball.

This and the other photographs in the book were taken in the Championship Court at Wembley, where the back wall is made of glass to enable the spectators to have a clearer view of the game.

further towards the back wall, so that the angle of the racket has to be turned still further. This is now the position for the worst problem of all, the ball in the back corner, where your normal swing is prevented by the closeness of the back wall. You now place your feet in this 'reverse' position, with your leading foot towards the back corner in question, and the other so placed that your feet and body are facing the opposite back corner. You are now clear of

The player is shown just after the moment of impact. Being well clear of the side wall, the player can get maximum leverage, and with the open face to the racket, can ensure providing the upward direction necessary to make the ball carry to the front wall.

the back wall to swing freely, and by hitting the ball in front of the foot, and making maximum use of the wrist, the ball can be hit upwards on to the side wall in such a way that it will carry comfortably to the opposite front corner.

These then are the normal shots used during the rallies in Squash. Before we have a proper game, however, we must learn to serve. Although the service is the first shot in each rally, it is not an easy shot to learn first. It becomes much

This photograph shows the upward follow-through. The foot position shown facilitates the necessary quick movement back to the 'T'.

The correct way to play
a high volley; the racket
head is well up and
following through high,
and the wrist is locked.

easier once the ordinary lob and drive have been mastered.
Before beginners practise service and return of service, it is
necessary to have discussed the problem of retrieving from
the rear corners as the aim of the service is to hit the ball
precisely there. The service also has a large number of rules
and regulations, and we need to understand the use of all
the lines on the floor and the centre line on the front wall.
The next chapter will be devoted to the service and return
and the rules connected with them, but I want to end this
chapter with just a word about volleying, as this is a much
used method of returning service.

The wrong way to finish a high volley. The racket head has been pulled down and the wrist turned over, with the result that the ball will be hit into the tin.

You will notice in this chapter that I have made no reference to volleying at all. The reason is that all the shots I have described can be played either as ground shots or volleys. However, it is not as easy to play some shots on the volley as others, and as a volley covers everything from about ten feet in the air to a couple of inches above the floor, there are, so to speak, volleys and volleys! The foot and body positions are basically the same and the drives and lobs are played in much the same way. However, angles are much less easy to control when played on the volley, and drops more difficult still. Indeed, the winner in the front of the court is not now 'guided' into the side-wall nick via the front wall as before, it is 'punched'. The volley in Squash is a full shot; the ball will not just rebound happily off a stationary racket, it will drop on your toe. It must be struck with a proper back-swing and follow-through, and it is especially important to keep the follow-through high. If the racket head drops, or is pulled downwards, the ball will go into the tin. It is a common fault of beginners to 'fly-swat' high shots, so that the ball is either hit into the roof or on to the floor, depending on which bit of the swing is in operation when the ball is struck; there is only a brief moment when the racket is in the right position to get the ball back properly. This highlights the basic difference between volleying and ground shots; in the latter, the wrist is used a great deal, in the former, it should be 'locked', and this is why it is risky to play angles on the volley, as these require use of the wrist.

You now have all the basic information to enable you to serve and return well, and it is time we dealt with this in detail.

3
How to score – the service and return

Before we discuss the way to serve, it is necessary to explain the scoring system in Squash, as this affects the service directly and indirectly. Most Squash matches consist of the best of five games, rather as Wimbledon matches are the best of five sets. A game in Squash is won by the first player to reach nine points. However, if the score reaches eight points all, the player not serving at that moment must choose whether the game is won by the player reaching nine first, as before, in which case he elects 'No set', or whether the winner will be the first to reach ten points, when he chooses 'Set two'. A point is scored by a player when he wins a rally in which he served; if he loses that rally, the score remains as it was, but his opponent takes over the service. As a result, in a close match the service can alternate for quite a long time with very few points being scored. It is customary to announce the score with the server's points called first.

It will be as well to learn the correct Squash terms; the server is known as 'Hand-in' and the receiver as 'Hand-out', and the period during which one player is serving is known as a 'Hand'. Thus one can say that a particular player won five points in one hand, which would mean that he won five rallies, and thus scored five points, without losing a rally and so conceding the right to serve. It now becomes clear that a good service is vital, because if you can serve a winner, or at least gain the initiative by forcing a defensive shot from your opponent, it helps to score points. It seems unintelligent not to bother about the service – and very many players, even at the top level, do not do so – when you are risking throwing away the rally and with it your right to serve and to score points. It is equally vital to have a safe return of service, and not to present your opponent with a point by missing it every time it gets near the back corners, or by scooping it out into the middle of the court. Your return of service should be able to be aggressive against an indifferent service, and sound enough to get into the rally on level terms against even the most accurate of serves.

Let us now look at the rules governing the service. The right to serve at the beginning of a match is decided by the spin of a racket, and thereafter Hand-in retains the service until he loses a rally. This means that after winning a game he starts serving first in the next game. He may elect to start serving from whichever side he likes every time he becomes Hand-in or starts a game, but while he remains Hand-in, he must serve from alternate sides with each new rally. He will obviously elect to start serving into his opponent's weaker side, and unless he finds out to the contrary, he should assume this to be the backhand.

The service itself is complicated; to be correct, three requirements have to be satisfied, and there are various ways in which the service can be adjudged a 'single' fault, and others which constitute a kind of 'double' fault in the one shot. If the service is correct the rally is on, and Hand-out has to return the ball. If it is one of the forms of a 'single' fault, Hand-out may choose whether to accept it or not. If he does accept it, the rally is in progress, just as if the service had been correct, but if he does not, then Hand-in has a second service, and if this is another fault of any kind, he becomes Hand-out. If Hand-in serves one of the 'double' faults, he becomes Hand-out straight away. I have used the terms single and double in inverted commas to try to clarify the situation, because most people will know what I mean by the Tennis terms. In Squash Hand-in is said to have served a fault (for a single) and to have served his hand out (for a double).

For Hand-in to serve correctly, he must avoid serving a footfault, hit the ball directly to the correct part of the front wall, and it must then rebound to land in the opposite rear quarter of the court. In detail, he must stand with at least one foot correctly grounded within the service-box area. The service boxes are the little squares on either side of the court, just behind the 'short' line, which divides the court into a front and back area. To be 'correctly grounded', the foot must be in contact with the floor as the ball is struck; just a toe on the floor is enough, but no part of the foot may be in contact with any of the lines or the floor outside the box. The other foot may also be in the box, or it can be absolutely anywhere else. The ball must then be thrown in the air by the non-racket hand and struck by the racket before it bounces or hits a wall, and then go direct to the front wall, and hit it below the out-of-court line at the top and above the 'cut' line in the centre of the front wall. Note that 'on' a line is wrong in Squash, whether it is one of the floor lines or one of those on the wall. The ball must then rebound so that it bounces in any part of the whole back quarter of the court opposite to the service box from which Hand-in has delivered the ball. This is the area enclosed by the short line and the 'half court line', which runs from the centre of the short line to the centre of the back wall. In Squash, Hand-out is allowed to volley the service if he wishes, and in fact he will do so very frequently. In the same way that he makes a single fault good by taking it, he also makes it good by volleying it, whether or not it would have landed in the correct area. For receiving service, Hand-out is allowed to stand wherever he likes, and we will be discussing later the best place for him to be.

The 'single' fault can be produced in one of three ways. Hand-in may serve a footfault; he may hit the ball against the front wall on or below the cut line, as long as it is above the tin; or the ball may rebound from the front wall and land on the floor anywhere other than inside the opposite back corner of the court. Any combination of these in the one shot only counts as one single fault, but any two consecutive faults count as a double, and lose Hand-in the service, whether or not it is the same error that has been repeated. Thus a footfault, with the ball going on to hit the front wall below the cut line and then bounce on the incorrect area of the floor is a single fault, but a footfault, not taken by Hand-out, followed by a service in which the ball bounces in the wrong part of the court, is a double fault, and the right to serve changes hands.

The crimes which constitute a 'double' fault in the one shot fall into three categories. Firstly, any shot which does not at least reach the front wall correctly above the board, loses the service. This includes a complete failure to hit the ball, any mishit which hits the ball into the floor or the tin, any incorrect service in which the ball has been bounced on the floor or wall before being hit, or any 'double hit'. The latter occurs sometimes when the racket does not make clean contact with the ball, and follows through and strikes it again. Secondly, any shot which is out of court is a double fault, as is, thirdly, a service in which the ball hits a side wall on its way to the front wall.

So much for what a service may and may not do; let us now discuss how the shot should be played. In Tennis and Table Tennis, a server can make use of the weapons of power, swerve and spin, but in Squash the need to hit the ball against the front wall rules them out. The ball can, of course, be hit hard, but the wall removes any chance of blasting the ball past the opponent, like the cannonball service on a Tennis court. Similarly, any spin or swerve imparted to the ball by the racket will be 'absorbed' by the wall, and the ball will then rebound and bounce in a straight line. The only real weapon for Hand-in is accuracy, which entails a lot of practice. There are two basic types of service, the lob and the drive. The lob is the attacking shot which if played well will put the opponent under pressure, may cause a mishit, and should guarantee a defensive return. This, in turn, retains the initiative for Hand-in by offering him a chance of an aggressive shot on the third stroke of the rally. The drive has not the same attacking potential, but is of great use when the lob would be a dangerous shot, if, for example, the court had a low roof, or the ball were particularly hot and fast, and liable to fly out of court, or if the score were such that Hand-in could not afford to take the slightest chance of hitting the ball out. The aim of the drive is to launch the rally safely and to restrict Hand-out's return to a fairly defensive shot.

As we saw when talking about the lob, the object of the high shot in Squash is to cause embarrassment in the back corners, and so it is with the lob type of service. It is obviously more difficult for the shot to be a winner as a service because the opponent is now in position waiting for it, whereas in the rally situation, he has had to run back from further up the court as the ball has been hit over his head. Against that, the lob service can be played from a standing position, with all the time in the world for the player to steady himself and take careful aim. He should therefore be able to produce greater accuracy than if he has had to play a lob in a rally, and has had to run to get to the ball in time. Also, he has not been able to select the height of the ball he wishes to lob in a rally, and if his opponent has just played a drop shot, the ball may be inconveniently low, but in a service situation he can choose his own most comfortable way to produce the stroke.

You will remember that we found one of the ways for taking speed off a lob was to ensure that it hit the side wall and the floor before reaching the back wall. The same goes for the lob service. Consequently, the further forward Hand-in can place himself in the service box, and the closer he can get to the side wall, the wider the angle he will be able to create on the front wall. Thus the ball will strike more directly against the side wall, and if allowed to reach the back wall, will tend to slide along it, and so not rebound far into the court. The object is to force Hand-out to take a ball dropping almost vertically in a position where he is impeded by the side and back walls. So take up a position where the ball can be struck comfortably in the

The correct position for
the forehand lob service,
standing well forward in
the service box and close
to the side wall. A line
through the toes would
lead to the point of aim
on the front wall. Eye on
ball as always.

front wall-side corner of the service box. This means that
the shot will be played on the forehand from the forehand
side, and on the backhand from the backhand side. The
latter may prove difficult at first for a beginner, but should
be practised until it can be done. The point of aim on the
front wall is just about the centre point of the panel between
the cut line and the out-of-court line; it is impossible to be
more precise as the exact point will vary from court to
court, ball to ball and player to player. The higher the
roof and the slower the ball, the further up the front wall
the contact point should be, but that centre point should

give you an initial target to aim at. The ball should be
struck underarm and upwards on to the front wall, so that
it continues upwards to reach its highest point about a
third of the way down the court, and then falls to strike the
side wall just below the out-of-court line a few feet behind
the rear line of the service box. Again, the exact position
will vary slightly with circumstances. The ball should then
drop on the floor and 'die' close to the rear wall, either just
before or after hitting it. The foot position for this shot is
slightly different from the orthodox mid-rally position;
place the feet so that the line through the toes (that is a
line from the tip of the rear shoe to the tip of the front shoe)
should lead to the central position on the front wall. Throw
the ball into the air with the non-racket hand, and hit it
with an upward, easy swing to the front wall. It is not a
hard hit shot; the ball is made to carry to the back by its
upward flight, not by being slammed hard at the front wall.

The other type of service, the drive, is produced in a
completely different way. Whereas the aim for the lob was
to widen the angle on the front wall, the aim for the drive
service is to narrow it as much as possible, in order to bring
the ball back from the front wall as nearly as possible
parallel to the side wall. To do this, the ball is struck as far
towards the centre of the court as can be achieved comfortably, which means that the shot is played as a backhand
from the forehand side of the court, and vice versa. The
rear foot should be left behind to observe the footfault rule,
and the other placed towards the centre of the court. The
ball is again thrown in the air and hit by a normal drive
action towards the front wall. This time the point of aim is
three quarters of the way across the front wall, and some
two or three feet above the cut line; once again the exact
position has to be determined by the speed of the ball. The
ball should be played so that it strikes the side wall in the
most difficult place for the receiver, and this will vary
according to how he likes to take service. If he is standing
well back, the ball can be aimed at the side wall several feet
behind the rear service box line, but if he is standing well

The correct position for the defensive service, struck on the backhand from the forehand side of the court. The rear foot is just within the service box, and the leading foot as far across court as comfortable.

forward, try to make the ball hit the side wall level with
where he has placed himself. He will not choose to take the
ball at the length he originally intended, if at that point the
ball is in contact with the side wall, so he will be forced to
move forward or back, and may well be forced into error.
As this type of service is played with Hand-in facing across
the court, he can see exactly where his opponent is, and
aim the shot accordingly. With the lob service, Hand-in's
back is to his opponent, but in this case it does not matter;
the importance then is the accuracy of the service. If a lob
service is good, it will be good wherever the opponent has
decided to stand, but a drive service is at its best when
geared to the position of the opponent. Once again, it is not
a hard shot; accuracy counts far more than horse power.

These are the only two types of service that you should
concern yourself with in the early stages of Squash. Indeed,
they are the only worthwhile regular types of service
anyway. There are other ways of serving, and if one of
these is slipped in occasionally, especially if the opponent is
not too alert, you may get a winner by surprising him.
The ball can be hit hard and overarm, as in Tennis; it can
be served straight down the centre of the court, just the
appropriate side of the half court line. Alternatively, it
can be hit high and hard at the front wall on the server's own
side of the court so that it rebounds diametrically off the
near side wall and across court. However, if the opponent
has his wits about him, the hard-hit shot must present him
with an easy return at some stage, as it bounces off walls
and rebounds into the clear part of the court. Furthermore,
any shot arriving across court from the server's own side,
or down the centre, ensures that the server has to stay on
that side to avoid the risk of being hit by the ball, which
opens up an awful lot of the court into which Hand-out
can attempt a winning return. So concentrate on the two
main types, and remember above all that it is worthwhile
developing a really good service. Do not just stroll into the
service box and give it a swipe on your way; settle down,
think about which service you think will be best in all the

circumstances of court, ball, score and opponent, take up the correct position and play a deliberate and accurate shot.

Now let us discuss the return of service. If the service is the most important shot in any rally, because after all, no rally can be without one, and it tends to set the tone for what follows, then the second most important shot is the return of service. However brilliant a player's other shots are, he will not be able to use them effectively if he surrenders the initiative, whether Hand-in or Hand-out, by having a poor service and an uncertain return. If at all possible, you should try to gain the initiative from your own service, or from your return of the other person's service, but in any event you should be able to guarantee reaching the third shot of each rally at least on level terms. As the receiver of the service you begin with certain advantages; you know where the service is coming to, you can stand where you like to receive it, you have a long time to watch it on its way and judge the best point at which to meet it with your racket. Many Hand-outs, however, handicap themselves by standing in the wrong place, and by not taking advantage of the time interval between the service actually being struck and the ball arriving in the back corner.

It is obvious that the service will not arrive every time at exactly the right place for you to hit the ball without moving, so as movement is going to be necessary, let us make sure it is in the most convenient direction. To the average human being this is forwards rather than backwards, and running backwards is even more hazardous than usual when there is a wall behind you! So to start with, stand close to the back wall and in the centre of the court corner of the area into which the service is coming. Your movement will then be forwards and towards the side wall. If you stand too far up the court, and Hand-in hoists a good lob service at you, you will be groping your way backwards, not knowing when you or your racket are going to hit the back wall. Remember, too, that a ball hitting a wall direct will rebound further from it than one which bounces on the floor first, so it is important to know whether the service is going to hit the wall or floor first. If I were to ask you to guess accurately where a ball was going to hit a wall, if I were to throw the ball from a range of ten yards, you would automatically go and stand by the wall, not by me or halfway along. Therefore if you stand near the rear wall initially, you will be able to judge the flight of the ball much more accurately, and be able to decide in good

The correct position for the receiver in the backhand side of the court, waiting to move forward and to his left to intercept the service before it can become dangerous in the back corner. He is watching the server to give himself maximum anticipation time, and his racket is up and ready.

time whether it can be left to hit the wall and rebound into the wide open spaces, or whether it has to be intercepted before it comes dangerously close to the back wall. Obviously, as you gain experience at the game, you will be able to make this assessment from further up the court, but you will learn more quickly if you start at the back of the court. The advantage of moving forward to take the service earlier is that you can punish a poor service more quickly and severely. By the same argument we used when talking about drop shots, when we agreed that it was easier to be accurate over a short rather than a long distance, it is clear that it will be easier to play an attacking volley, or whatever other aggressive shot is being attempted, from a position further up the court. Against a good server, this forward position can never be as far up as the rear corner of the service box, so it is not a very long move anyway.

The types of return depend on the service and your own stronger strokes. For a poor service, you may of course use whatever shot you like; it is just like a winner being presented to you at any stage in the rally. To return a good service, however, is not so simple. The safe shots are ones which keep the ball close to the side walls and in the corners of the court. Consequently, the shot down the side wall is probably the best. Like all shots aimed at being good length strokes parallel with the wall, you have two 'bites of the cherry'; the ball may stay awkwardly close to the wall, or die in the back corner, or both. Returning service is a good time to avail yourself of these advantages. The shot may be hit hard and, if it is accurate, can be most effective. It will force your opponent into the back corner, as he will be unable to cut it off in mid-court. However, the important thing is the accuracy rather than the speed. If you sacrifice accuracy merely to hit hard, you are simply putting the ball back on your opponent's racket while you yourself are still out of position. If the service has been a particularly good one, you will quite possibly not find yourself in a clear enough position in the court to have a sufficiently full swing to hit the ball hard. If in doubt, play the ball high and softly down the wall and be safe. Frequently it will be necessary to volley the service, but the same aims hold as for ground stroke returns; simply remember to volley with a 'locked' wrist, and refrain from fly-swatting. If a high volley is needed, see that the racket head follows through high, and is not dragged down or across as this will have the same effect on the ball itself.

Another useful return of service is the cross-court lob, again played either after the ball has bounced or as a volley, although the latter is more difficult to play accurately. The lob can be a deliberate shot or one forced on you when the ball is dropping short and you are having to stretch for it. You will remember we found that one of the ways of hitting the ball across court was to strike it in front of the leading foot; if now you are forced into just that position, then make a virtue out of necessity, and play the ball across court quite deliberately as a lob.

If the service is a really perfect one, or you have made an error of judgement in your approach to the ball, you may be forced to pick it up out of the corner and will have no option but to 'boast' the ball out via the side wall. This is bound to mean that the ball will travel to the opposite front corner, and if you stand around too long after playing the shot your opponent will be able to get up and play a winning drop shot. So, as soon as you have played your boast, set off at full speed to cover this danger.

Remember then that the service and the return of service are the most vital shots in any rally and it is well worth the time and effort required to make sure that yours are accurate.

4
Court craft and tactics

So far we have discussed stroke production in some detail, but have only touched on the very vital questions of movement around the court and basic tactics. Squash is a very energetic and physically demanding game, and later on, when you come to play matches you will realize that often the difference between a winner and a loser is the ability to keep going longest. But one often sees a less fit, more experienced player finish up by beating a younger, fitter opponent, simply by making the latter run all over the court, while being economical in his own movements.

A number of ingredients go towards skilful use of court craft. Clearly, if you can anticipate where your opponent is going to hit the ball, and be moving early in that direction, you will not have to move as quickly to get there. This is partly experience, partly an intelligent assessment of an opponent's type of game and likely shots, but mainly a matter of watching the ball right on to the opponent's racket, so that you get the maximum amount of time to see what shot he is playing and thus where the ball will go. Also, it is much easier to move off in any direction to retrieve the opponent's shot from a position in the centre of the court. Two things that are very difficult are retrieving a well-struck shot from any other position than in the centre of the court, and being forced to change direction completely when the opponent has played the ball back into the corner of the court that you are currently moving away from. It is therefore absolutely vital to get back to the centre of the court—the 'T' area where the lines join—after every stroke including the service, and to get there, poised to move off, before the opponent can possibly play his shot. If you do this, you deny him any wide open spaces or obvious target areas at which to hit the ball.

Thirdly, it is important to avoid unnecessary exertion yourself. A very famous coach once said that he never 'ran' around the court, he 'moved', and there is a great deal in that. By good anticipation, and correct positioning, he did not have to charge about; he was able to 'move' into the best place to play the ball, and back again to the 'T'. The extra time he gave himself allowed him to get into the basic position from which to play all the shots, and so could use his full range. If you think about it, that 'stance' that we

The correct position to take a ball close to the wall; balance is right and racket head is up, with the eyes right over the shot. The player has moved the minimum distance from the 'T', and after the shot can move back again in two strides with little effort.

have settled on enables you to reach to the side walls, and
the corners of the court without actually going there and it
is the easiest position from which to move back to the
centre of the court. Again, this emphasizes the point about
playing shots with the racket head up and not trailing; the
person who plays with his racket head down by his feet

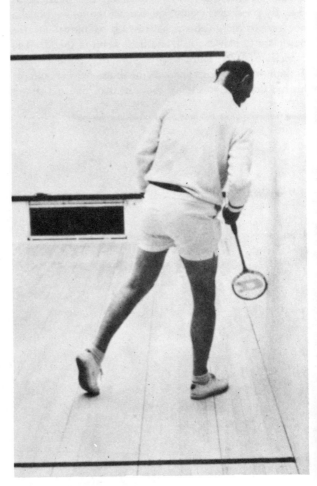

Wrong position to take a
ball close to the wall.
Racket is in a trailing
position, arm has little
control, and the player
has not only taken an
entire step away from the
'T', but has to take an
extra step back, and is not
sufficiently on balance to
make this easy.

has to move much closer to the ball than the player who is hitting the ball well away from himself. So the 'trailer' has an extra step to take to and from the ball every time he plays a shot. Multiply those extra steps by the number of shots in the rally and rallies in the match, and he will be seen to be covering a lot more ground—and all of it unnecessary as well as tiring.

I want to say a word now about speed around the court. Beginners do not find it easy to judge what difficult shots are in fact retrievable, and give up going for balls that a more experienced player would reach comfortably. This is partly due to faulty anticipation through lack of experience, but mainly the result of not realizing what they are capable of. If you watch a major championship, and listen to the involuntary gasps of the spectators, you will find that these are more frequently for a brilliant piece of retrieving than for an outstanding shot. The shots seem to be taken for granted; everyone can play most of them, and it is merely a polished version of the club player's shots that the champions produce. One admires the skill and accuracy, but is not staggered by them. It is when a champion gets to a ball that the average player would not have reached that the crowd roars. So right from the start, attempt to reach the ball, even when you think there is no chance at all of doing so. You will be surprised at how often a quick dart, a full-stretch lunge and a despairing flick of the racket will scrape the ball back into play. Remember, too, that the same speed is necessary when returning to the 'T' as when moving to the ball.

Moving from speed about the court to the speed of the rallies, we come to another failure of inexperienced players. They tend to try to hit the ball too hard too often, and do not vary the speed of the rally. This ties up with my comments about anticipation; if a player can be pretty sure what his opponent is going to do, he can confidently stand in the part of the court where he knows the ball will come, or can move there in an unhurried way. Too frequently, it is possible to stroll about in the area three quarters of the way back from the front wall, because almost every shot is being hit there, and even when something is attempted in the front of the court, it is being hit at almost the same speed and is no trouble to get to. On the other hand, if genuine softly played drops and angles are being fairly evenly mixed in with the drives and lobs, the opponent has to come up to cover the danger of winners in the front corners and will be more vulnerable to the length shots. Remember, therefore, to vary the shots, change the pace of the rallies and do not let your opponent settle into any sort of rhythm.

Now two points about defensive tactics. There will be times when you have been forced to play a completely defensive shot, such as a boast from a back corner, and your opponent has been presented with a very easy shot in the front of the court. Obviously he is in an excellent position to play a winner, and should do so, but you can minimize his chances of success by coming right up the court and waiting behind him, ready to cover a drop or angle shot in the front of the court. If he does produce one of these shots, you have a good chance of returning it, and even, if it is a bad one, of hitting a winner past him. If, on the other hand, he has heard you come up close behind him, he may decide not to take the risk of this happening, and may drive or lob the ball. Again, this may be such a well-placed shot that it is a winner, but it may not be, especially if your approach has made him change his mind. There is the possibility that a drive may rebound from the back wall far enough to give you a chance of returning it, and a lob is a long time in the air and gives you a few seconds grace. The point to remember is that if you are too far back in the court, all you will get is a good view of a drop or angle shot bouncing twice in the front corners, but even if you are too far up, there is a fair chance of picking up any shot hit past or over you.

The second point is that you should never try to hit yourself out of trouble. This applies anywhere in the court, but in particular to positions in front of the short line, and near the side walls. If you are off balance or really stretching for a shot, it is unlikely that you will be able to play any stroke at all accurately, so it is vital to do all you can to get the rally back on an even keel; it is dangerous to attempt any 'touch' shot, such as a drop, and likely to be fatal to hit the ball hard. Apart from the chance of hitting an uncontrolled shot into the roof or the tin, the likelihood is that you will hit the ball back to your opponent too quickly for your own good. If he is in position in the centre of the court and you hit the ball hard and within his reach, you will not have given yourself a chance to recover before he can place the ball well away to the other side of the court for a winner. The only solution is to hit the ball high, and use the time while the ball is in mid-air and so out of your opponent's reach, to get back to the 'T' position. So lob yourself out of trouble, in the front of the court in particular.

Perhaps it would be helpful to finish with a list of headings of the various topics we have discussed to help you do the right things when you start playing games.

1 Take care and time over every service.
2 Stand well back and move forward to receive service.
3 Keep your eye on the ball all the time, especially when it is behind you.
4 Move to the 'T' position after every shot including the service.
5 Move towards the centre of the court first, then up or down to the 'T', if hitting the ball back into the same quarter of the court.
6 Use the full range of strokes in your repertoire.
7 Keep the racket head up in all strokes and as you move round the court.
8 Try for every ball; you will surprise yourself.
9 Lob yourself out of trouble.
10 Always cover the short shots in the front of the court by moving well up behind your opponent.

5
Practice

Practice makes perfect, and nowhere is the old saying more true than in Squash. There are many things which help improve your play, but whatever else you do, in the final analysis, you have got to put in your time on court. Your rate of improvement is certain to be geared very closely to the number of times you actually strike a Squash ball with a Squash racket against a Squash court wall.

Other things that will help, if used intelligently, are coaching, watching top-class matches, seeing instructional films, playing different types of opponent, discussing the game with knowledgeable players, and of course reading Squash books and magazines. All can be helpful and interesting, and all help to break up the monotony of solid practice, but none is a replacement for it. And remember, I said 'if used intelligently'. People can make mistakes in their use of aids like coaching. Coaches are only human and may, with the best intentions in the world, give advice which is normally sound, but happens not to suit your particular case. Do not rely solely on one coach, or on one coaching book; if you have only one coach or book, bear in mind that much of what is said will be of help, but some things may not suit *you*. It is only too easy for a beginner to believe in the infallibility of a well-known coach, and to be groomed in a style which is not right for him. It is equally easy to make the mistake of attending course after course, and going from coach to coach, under the fond illusion that the more instruction you have, the better player you will be. Remember that the aim is to become a good match player, and when you get into your first match, none of your coaches will be there to make your brain think the right things or hold your hand as you play a drop shot. You, with their help, must get yourself to the correct state of mental and physical readiness and of technical ability, in order to be able to stand on your own feet when up against an opponent. A coach is there to answer questions, to show you how to practise, to prevent bad habits developing, to criticize your failings and encourage your improvement, to explain the rules and tactics and in general to guide you along the right road. He may guide, but you have to supply the movement along that road, and your progress will only come by spending time on court. So use your coach and coaching aids intelligently, and similarly watch matches intelligently. It is rather like a learner driver situation; most learners have often watched other people driving cars, but when it comes to learning how to drive, very little of the art of handling a car has rubbed off on to them. Once they begin to learn, they thus watch a driver much more intelligently to see exactly what he is doing and why. It is the same with Squash. I have known club players who have watched a match without really being aware of anything but the score. They would simply not have noticed, for example, that one player was noticeably weaker on the backhand or that his opponent was especially strong at the forehand drop shot. If they had been watching in order to learn something as well as to enjoy the game, they could have spotted faults to avoid and strong points to imitate; they could have tried to work out the tactics of the two players, and how these changed as the game progressed. Squash is a thinking game and it is never too early to realize that and to devote a little thought to it.

Practice, the importance of which I am stressing, must also be approached in an intelligent way. It is not simply a question of going on court and slamming a ball around until you get fed up. It is only too easy to become fed up if the whole thing is aimless. You are then doing yourself active harm, rather than any good. If you feel bored, then pack up the practice for the day and go and do something else. However, practice does not need to be boring at all; it can be made very interesting and encouraging, as well as good fun, and I want to suggest some ways in which you can not only practise the various shots but also enjoy yourself. I tend to divide practice into three types; there is practice on your own, practice with a coach and practice with a friend. Each has its place, and the time to be spent on each will depend on your own personality and your own opportunities. Personality comes into it because not everyone has the patience and dedication to practise sensibly on his own for any length of time, whereas there are individuals who gain far more by themselves than when distracted by someone else. Opportunity dictates how often you have the chance of receiving coaching or of going on a court with a friend also keen to practise.

Practice on your own has advantages and limitations. It has the advantage of allowing you to do exactly what you want to do and not having to share the time with anyone else. It has the disadvantage of limiting you to accuracy and stamina practice, because there is no other person to reproduce the match situation of someone else hitting the ball to you. Even so, it can be useful to 'groove' a particular shot, and repeat it *ad nauseam* until it is right. One of the dangers of practising alone is that the ball can very easily become cold. If, for example, you are trying to practise lob services, it is necessary to keep hitting the ball up and down hard several times every few minutes or your practice will be useless. You may get a splendid service going, but the ball will be slower than it ever would be in a proper game, and so when you come to reproduce the service you have been perfecting with a ball of match speed, you will find it will fly straight into the roof. I personally prefer to practise certain accurate strokes on my own. For instance, it is a bit soul-destroying for someone else if you keep on hitting the ball up and down the side wall to yourself. However, if you want to practise hitting the ball close to the wall, it is irritating to have to keep hitting it to a partner who wants to try out angles. So this is a shot you can usefully practise alone. Stand well back in the court, and see how often you can play the ball on that particular 'wing', i.e. forehand or backhand, between yourself and the near wall. The aim is to make the ball cling as close as possible to the wall as it comes back from the front, and to be heading for a good length in the back corner. When you can do this satisfactorily, you can try doing it again with a series of volleys, or of alternate drives and volleys. Remember to get into the correct position each time, and try to analyse what went wrong, if and when something does go wrong.

It is possible to practise any shot on your own by hitting the ball up to the front wall and playing that particular shot as it returns. This does have disadvantages, however, because apart from the need to keep the ball warmed up to match speed, there is the drawback that you yourself have hit the previous shot and so know how fast the ball will be approaching, and from what direction. It is all right just to get the shot technically right, but it will still need practice with someone else hitting the ball to you, preferably in a rally situation. It is useful to perfect the art of getting the ball out of the back corners on your own. You can plant your feet in the right place initially and then throw the ball with the free hand on to the walls, and play your boast as it emerges. Alternate the walls so that the ball sometimes hits the side wall first and sometimes the back, so that you get used to gauging which way it will rebound. Do not try and bounce it on the floor first; from a position as close to the corner as you now are, it will just not bounce out again far enough to be returned. As you become more proficient from the static position, move a little further away, and again lob the ball by hand into the corner, hitting the walls first as before. From this distance, your throw will not be quite as accurate, and you will have to move into the correct position in order to hit the ball. There will be some initial failures, and you should analyse after each exactly what went wrong. Were you too near to the ball, did you hit it too hard into the side wall and not high enough, and so on. Once you can achieve consistent success in both back corners, you are ready to move back to the 'T', throw the ball into either corner and move back at match speed to retrieve it. It is essential to practise this shot and become completely safe in the back corners. If you are not, then your opponents will not need to worry about producing any brilliant angles or drops, and need take no chances at all. They merely need to drive and lob into the rear corners to exploit your weakness. Furthermore, it is a weakness that will let you down badly on receiving service, and will present your opponents with many cheap points.

There is one other danger which affects practice on your own, and that is that bad habits can easily begin, and if repeated often enough, be very difficult to correct later. No one can see himself producing a stroke, and so cannot see how well or badly he is doing it. You can only judge on results; a shot that returns a ball successfully from a static position, may well not be correct enough to return it under the pressure of a match. In the match situation, it will be necessary to move into position and to play that shot against the hostile and well-placed stroke of an 'enemy'. So do seek advice from time to time from a coach, or a friend who is a good player, and check that you are on the right lines.

I have not yet mentioned the need to be very physically fit for playing Squash. You may find that once you begin playing proper games your legs and lungs, not to mention a few muscles you did not know you had, will be suffering. You can use individual practice to improve both speed and stamina by playing rallies all over the court and cheating like mad. You can sentence yourself to 'time' rallies, as opposed to rallies ended by an incorrect shot, and ignore balls that go out, hit the tin or bounce twice; just carry on as though they had been good, until the time is up, or you collapse. Just a word of warning to the not-so-young, or people who used to play Squash but have not done so for some years; start gently. If you were taking up swimming, you would not dive in from the top board, or try to swim the Channel on your first couple of dips. And yet you see middle-aged characters go on court for the first time and try to recapture their youth by leaping all over the court to the accompaniment of twanging hamstrings and Achilles tendons!

Let us now consider ways in which you and a friend can help each other when a coach is not available. We have already discussed the early practices of keeping rallies going up and down or across court. You can now extend these to exercise any of the shots in a game situation, and you can act as coaches for each other. I will talk about the latter first, as it is useful to get the strokes as good as possible in a semi-static situation before going on to the mobile practices. Basically a coach should 'feed' the ball so that his pupil can play the particular stroke being exercised, so this is what you and your friend can do. Let us suppose that the drop shot is the shot in question; the 'pupil' goes to the 'T', where he would be in a match, preparatory to moving up and playing a drop. The acting coach places himself near the side wall where the drop will finish up, and plays the ball into the centre of the front quarter of the court. The pupil moves forward and plays the drop and returns to the 'T', and the friend repeats the process. It may be necessary for him to play an extra stroke himself in between drops, or the pupil will not have time to do the return trip to the 'T'; in a match, no one will be standing waiting for the shot so he would have time to complete the manoeuvre. It is also good to make the pupil realize that part of the practice for any shot is the movement to the ball and away from it again afterwards. This is what I meant by 'semi-static'. Static is when you are merely standing in the correct position 'grooving' a stroke. Semi-static is when you are practising the one shot, but moving into position for it, and away again.

For the ordinary angle shots, the pupil again stands near the 'T', ready to move up and play the angle from the centre of the front quarter. For the forehand angle, the acting coach stands across court in the front backhand quarter, where the ball will come, and places the ball back into a suitable place for the next angle. There is one point to remember about this practice; we agreed that angles are deceptive shots, played in contrast to what the opponent will be expecting, and therefore no warning must be given of the new intention. If, therefore, the angle is in contrast to an expected drop, it will still be played as a gentle shot and rolled round the body as the opponent comes up for the drop. If the contrast is to the hard drive down the wall, then the angle will also be hit harder and will go right across court to the opposite side wall. The friend should place himself accordingly, and remember that once again an extra shot from the friend will be necessary to allow the pupil to get back to the centre of the court.

The reverse angle is practised in a similar way; this time the acting coach takes up position near the closer side wall, and plays the ball into the centre of his own front quarter of the court. His partner can then come up and pull it across to the opposite side wall, and so back towards him. This shot is almost invariably a hard-hit stroke, in contrast to the hard cross-court drive. The cross-court drop is not frequently used, and is in itself a surprise shot for when the opponent would be expecting a straight drop; in this situation a reverse angle would be of no use, since it would come back to where the opponent was expecting the straight drop in the first place.

For practising the back-corner boasts, your friend can stand in the back corner of the court and drop the ball in front of himself, and so study the production of the stroke from close quarters, and he can then, from a position in mid-court, throw the ball into the corner to allow you to move to it and retrieve it. This can then lead to mutual practice between the two players of the lob and boast. Taking it in turns, one has a spell of concentrated lobbing, while the other boasts the ball back. Thus the rally is continuing on a course from one front corner into the dia-

metrically opposite back corner. Both players have to return to the 'T' between shots, but the one in the front of
the court must be particularly careful to watch behind him
as he returns to the centre of the court, as he would need
to do in a match.

The drives to a good length down the side wall can also
be usefully practised in this way; one player restricts himself to drives from the front corners, while his partner continues to boast from the back. This adds mobility to the
practice, which is not possible with the lob type we have
just covered, because the boasts are now returning the ball
to the opposite front corner from which the drive was hit,
and the next drive will return to the other back corner.
The final extension of this practice is when the player in the
rear of the court is allowed to practise producing drop
shots towards the front corners when the length of his
opponent's previous shot has not required a boast. The
two things to remember in these practices are that each
player must have his turn at the front, doing the lob and
drive practice, and at the back playing boasts and drops. In
the case of the lob versus boast practice, remember that
there are two diagonal lines across a court; the practice is
only half complete when you have had the forehand lob
against the backhand boast. Now switch to the backhand
lob and the forehand boast.

Perhaps the best way of practising the service and return
of service is to play a perfectly normal game, except that
the players only score points if these are earned off the
first two shots of the rally. In other words, if the service is
not returned, the server scores a point as usual; if the service
is a 'double' fault, or the receiver makes a winning return,
then he scores. If the service is good and the return correct,
but not a winner, the rally continues. Neither player scores,
and the only importance of the rest of that rally is to deter-
mine who serves at the start of the next rally. In this way,
the players really do concentrate on the service and return
as the only ways of scoring, but the rest of the rally is not
just a waste of time.

Let me, in conclusion, try to give you a few guide lines for practising.

1 Have a definite aim in view, and do not just hit the ball around aimlessly.
2 Try to perfect the production of a shot first before using it in a game situation.
3 Make sensible use of a coach and of coaching aids.
4 Always remember the safety angle and ensure that your strokes are 'controlled'.
5 Remember, when on your own, to keep the ball at match speed.
6 Make your practices competitive to add interest and reality to them.
7 Share the practices equally with your partner.
8 Practise the weaker parts of your game more than the strokes you find easiest.
9 Never continue practising if you become bored with it.
10 Try to vary your partners and play on different courts and with different speeds of ball in order to widen your experience.

I would only like to add that most players find ambition is the best spur to improvement. Most clubs have competitions within the club, and run several teams. Enter for the competitions and aim to be in one of the teams as soon as you can. Beyond the club, there are a great mass of tournaments in which you can compete. Your club, always

Your club, assuming it is under the auspices of the International Squash Rackets Federation, will give you guidance as to the organization of competition in your area and beyond

Most clubs nowadays have at least one coach among their members, and he will no doubt be glad to offer advice if you seek him out.

Be ambitious, play the game to win, and be successful, but above all enjoy it, and make sure that your opponent enjoys it as much as anyone can when he has just lost!